NEW PERSPECTIVES

The War in Kosovo

STEWART ROSS

WAYLAND

First published in 2000 by
Wayland Publishers Ltd,
61 Western Road,
Hove,
East Sussex BN3 1JD

This book was prepared for Wayland Publishers Ltd
by Ruth Nason.

Series editor: Alex Woolf
Series design: Stonecastle Graphics
Book design: Ruth Nason/Carole Design

Find Wayland on the internet at:
http://www.wayland.co.uk

British Library Cataloguing in Publication Data
Ross, Stewart
   The war in Kosovo. - (New perspectives)
   1.Yugoslav War, 1991 - Serbia - Kosovo - Juvenile
   literature 2.Kosovo (Serbia) - History - 20th century -
   Juvenile literature 3.Kosovo (Serbia) - Politics and
   government - Juvenile literature 4.Kosovo (Serbia) - Ethnic
   relations - Juvenile literature
   I.Title   949.7'1

ISBN 0 7502 2747 8

Printed in Hong Kong by Wing King Tong

Cover photos: a Kosovo
Liberation Army (KLA)
soldier sings as NATO
forces enter Kosovo,
July 1999; a mass funeral
of Kosovo Albanians killed
by Serb forces, 1998.

Page 1: A Kosovo Albanian
waits on a transit bus
taking refugees from a
border camp to a NATO
camp in Macedonia.

Acknowledgements

The Author and Publishers thank the following for their permission
to reproduce photographs: Camera Press: cover and pages 3, 4t, 5, 8,
10, 11t, 11b, 17b, 19b, 20, 21, 22, 23, 29, 33, 37t, 37b, 39, 40, 41, 46,
47, 50, 51, 53t, 54, 55, 56, 57; Howard Davies: pages 1, 34, 35, 52,
53b; Fototjenesten/Jan Kjaer: page 44; Hulton Getty: pages 15, 17t,
19t; Popperfoto: pages 4b, 7, 12l, 12r, 14, 25, 26, 27, 28, 30, 31, 32t,
32b, 38, 43, 45, 48, 49, 58, 59.

Publisher's note: Kosovo/Kosova
The Serbs use the spelling 'Kosovo', which has been the spelling
generally accepted in the US and UK. Albanian speakers, however,
know the province as 'Kosova', which is why you will find both
versions of the word in the documents in this book.

CONTENTS

The French air force prepares bombs at a NATO base in Italy.

THE FRENKIS

Quieter times: Kosovo
Albanians meet at a café
in Pec for coffee and a
chat, early 1980s.

March 1999: a Serbian
paramilitary runs for cover
during exchange of fire
with Kosovo Liberation
Army (KLA) guerrillas. The
KLA was determined to
drive the Serbs out of
Kosovo by force.

Pec is an ancient market town in western Kosovo. Standing on a small river between two mountain ranges, it displays a fascinating blend of Serbian and Albanian culture. The restored monastery, once the headquarters of the Serbian Orthodox Church, boasts fine frescoes and other treasures. The town centre has a more Oriental air, with narrow streets, mosques and Turkish-style houses. In normal times it is a wonderful place to visit.

But these are not normal times. It is late March 1999. Tank gunfire has reduced part of the town to ruins. Gangs of Serbian soldiers pass along the streets, kicking in the doors of houses and ordering the Albanian inhabitants to leave. They have five minutes – sometimes less – to get out.

Men, women and children, with a look of terror in their eyes, stagger into the street. A little girl clings to her teddy bear. Her mother clutches the family photographs, while her father struggles with the television. A soldier steps forward and points his rifle at the man, barking an order. For a second the man thinks about disobeying. Then he carefully lowers the television onto the road and turns to join his family. The soldier calls him back. No, he may not join his family. Tears fill his eyes as he is herded towards a group of men at the far end of the street.

The soldier returns to work. More terrified Albanian families are driven from their homes. Hundreds of women, children and old men join the long procession of refugees

on the long road towards the Albanian border. Younger men and professional people – doctors, lawyers, teachers – are marched to the sports stadium. Their fate is unknown.

That evening the Serbs set fire to the empty houses. Flames leap high into the night sky. The Albanian refugees, now huddled together in a field several miles away, stare at the orange glow in silence.

Refugees fled from Kosovo on foot or by car, truck or tractor. These people are arriving at the Kukes refugee camp on the Albanian border.

 ## Homes destroyed

Refugees from Pec claimed they had been attacked by Serb paramilitary (semi-official) soldiers known as 'Frenkis', after Frenki Simatovic, a former paramilitary leader. Arsim Kelmendi, a café owner, told Matthew McAlister of the US news-gathering service Newsday:

'Three nights ago paramilitaries in uniform – Frenkis – started to burn the roof of our neighbour. I went out to help him put it out, and they heard me and threw a grenade. One of my neighbours was wounded.'

Arsim's café was destroyed and then he fled, with many others, to the neighbouring region of Montenegro.

During the spring of 1999, the dreadful events of Pec were repeated all over the Yugoslav province of Kosovo. Serbian forces – units of the regular army, paramilitaries and police – moved through the countryside, shelling and burning towns and villages. Hundreds of thousands of Albanian refugees fled Yugoslavia. Others hid in woods and mountains. Many simply disappeared altogether.

Kosovo is a small but important region between Serbia and Albania. The majority of its population is Albanian. The Kosovo Albanians and the Serb minority are both deeply attached to the region.

The leader behind the Serb attacks was Slobodan Milosevic, President of Yugoslavia. His country consisted of three areas – Serbia, Montenegro and Kosovo. Serbia was the largest, inhabited largely by Serbs. In Montenegro, most of the Montenegrins spoke the same Serbo-Croat language as the Serbs and belonged to the same Eastern Orthodox Church. But the great majority of the population of the third and smallest area, Kosovo, were Albanian. They used the Albanian language and had their own customs and traditions. Many of them were Muslims.

For religious, historical and economic reasons, Kosovo was dear to Serb hearts. Milosevic and his supporters resented Albanian dominance there. Through the media they whipped up racist, anti-Albanian feelings. Milosevic promised to drive out the Albanians and restore Kosovo to the Serbs. He called this process 'ethnic cleansing'.

View from the West

Finding out what happened in Kosovo in 1999 is not easy, as the different sides gave out conflicting messages. The US State Department based this statement of 31 March 1999 on the accounts of refugees who had left Kosovo. Suava Reka is a town in southwest Kosovo.

'Suava Reka. On March 25, Serb forces massacred at least 30 Albanian Kosovars, most by burning them alive in their homes. Serb forces have reportedly killed over 100 civilians in the past week, and the town has been "cleansed" of its Albanian population.'

Other nations watched in horror as the ethnic cleansing gathered pace. Finally, after long negotiation and many warnings, on 24 March 1999 the Western allies of NATO launched air strikes against the Serbs. The Kosovo War had begun.

24 March 1999: the skyline of Kosovo's capital, Prishtina, is marked by tracers as NATO begins its air strikes.

View from Serbia

An 'Appeal to Refugees' on the Yugoslav government website blamed NATO attacks for the refugee crisis. Metohija is the western half of Kosovo.

'The Government of ... Yugoslavia calls on all citizens of Kosovo and Metohija not to leave their homes, their native areas and their state despite bombs, missiles and other cargoes of death which NATO has been unloading ... The Army and security forces of the Federal republic of Yugoslavia and Serbia are the staunchest defenders and protectors of all citizens and of all national communities ...'

ONE PLACE, MANY PEOPLES

Kosovo Albanian villagers show their support for independence from Serbia, April 1998.

Kosovo is a highland region in the troubled southeastern corner of Europe known as the Balkans. For much of the twentieth century, Kosovo was a province of Serbia. Serbia, in turn, was part of a much larger country, Yugoslavia, set up after the First World War (1914-18). Kosovo is bounded by Serbia in the northeast and northwest. To the west lie Montenegro, which is also part of Yugoslavia, and Albania. Kosovo's southern frontier is with Macedonia.

A ring of mountains separates Kosovo from its neighbours, and another smaller mountain range runs north-south across the province. The Serbs call the area to the west of these mountains Metohija, and the land to the east Kosovo. To most people, however, the name 'Kosovo' refers to the whole region. No part is below 365 metres (1,200 feet), which means that at night and in the winter it gets very cold. Snow lies on some of the mountains all year round.

The importance of Kosovo's mineral wealth

The official (Yugoslav) guide on the Yugoslav government website explains:

'In the [medieval] Serbian State ... the territory of Kosova became the central region, to which the greatest rise and fall of medieval Serbia was tied. Serbia experienced its most powerful economic rise after the middle of the 13th century with the development of mining – exploiting the mining centres in Kosovo.'

While most of Kosovo is given over to farming, it also contains some of the most valuable deposits of minerals in southeast Europe. These include lead, zinc, manganese, bauxite (the source of aluminium), chrome, iron, silver and coal. These riches have made Kosovo a target for invaders. For example, the ancient Romans occupied Kosovo for its wealth, as did the Germans during the Second World War. In our own times, one reason why the Serbs want to hold on to Kosovo is to control its mines.

Kosovo's position at the heart of the Balkans makes it strategically very important. The capital city, Prishtina, is at a key road junction on north-south routes, and control of Kosovo is vital for those seeking to dominate the whole area. For this reason, Kosovo has often been the scene of bitter fighting. For centuries it was fought over by Christians and the Muslim Ottoman Turks. In

On a plateau between high mountains, Kosovo occupies a key strategic position in the central Balkans. (See also the map on page 6.)

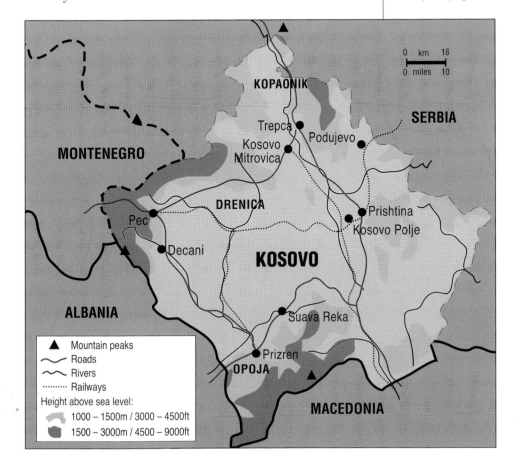

the twentieth century Serbian, Austro-Hungarian and German armies all suffered heavy losses in their vain struggle to hold on to the province. These lessons from history were not lost on the NATO commanders when they decided to get involved in Kosovo in 1999. They knew that turmoil in Kosovo threatened the peace of all southeast Europe and beyond.

A scaled-down Europe

Serbia, like all Balkan countries, is a vast mix of peoples and cultures.

'The 88,361 sq. km. of Serbia contain a scaled-down Europe. Had the Tower of Babel not been built where it had been, it would surely have been built in the heart of the Balkans, for Serbia is the meeting place of cultures, religions and languages. Although more than forty different nations live in Serbia, they do have some things in common – their homes are wide open to friends.' (Yugoslav Information Office website)

The people of Kosovo

The Kosovars belong to two main racial groups. The largest group (about 90 per cent in 1995) is of Albanian descent. No one is sure where the Albanian people came from. They seem to have been in the Balkan region for at least 2,000 years, and they may be descended from the Illyrians of Classical times. The 'Alb' part of their name is from the same root as the word 'Alps' and 'Alba' (the ancient name for Scotland), meaning 'mountain-land'.

Present-day Albanians – 'people from the mountains' – differ widely. Although Albania and Kosovo are their homelands, they are found all over the Balkan region, as well as in

January 1999: Kosovo Albanians demonstrate for independence, shouting 'We belong to Europe!'

Greece and Turkey. They speak the Albanian language. The majority are Muslims, but there are also Albanians who belong to the Christian Orthodox and Roman Catholic churches. There is little tradition of religious extremism in Kosovo. In the 1980s, many Muslims were prepared to support a party that called itself 'Christian Democrat'.

A gypsy family in Kosovo, January 1999.

Serbs make up most of the remaining 10 per cent of the population of Kosovo, although there are small numbers of other races. These include gypsies, Croats and Montenegrins. Like the Albanians, the Serbs are not a very exact racial group. Along with many other Balkan peoples, such as the Croats and Montenegrins, the Serbs are descended from the Slavs, who came to the Balkans from Asia in the fifth and sixth centuries AD. Scholars believe that the Serbs first began to settle in Kosovo in the late twelfth century.

The Russians, like the Serbs, also claim descent from the Slavs. For this reason the Serbs often look upon the Russians as their natural allies. During the 1999 war with NATO, for example, the Serb leader Slobodan Milosevic seems to have hoped that his Russian 'brothers' would come to his rescue.

Serb women in Montenegro protest against the NATO air strikes of 1999. They hold pictures of Milosevic and placards saying 'We are Yugoslav army too'.

Just as there are many Albanians living outside Albania, so there are Serbs living beyond Serbia. What most Serbs have in common, however, is the Serbo-Croat language, membership of the (Christian) Serbian Orthodox Church, and a long and troubled history. The region of Kosovo, sandwiched between Serbia and Albania and inhabited by both Serbs and Albanians, has sometimes played a very important part in that history.

Remembering the Battle of Kosovo: (right) June 1999: Patriarch Pavel of the Serbian Orthodox Church at the commemorative monument on the battlefield, after an open-air mass to mark the battle's 610th anniversary; (below) a Muslim guardian of the grave of Sultan Murat I.

The Battle of Kosovo

For long periods during the Middle Ages, Serbia (which included Kosovo) was a large and powerful state. In 1346, King Stefan Dusan actually called himself Tsar (or Emperor) of Serbia. By then, however, the Christian lands of eastern Europe, including Byzantium, Bulgaria and Hungary as well as Serbia, were under attack from the Ottoman Turks, who were Muslim.

On the morning of 15 June 1389, near Prishtina in central Kosovo, a largely Serb army led by Prince Lazar met an army under the command of the Turkish Sultan

Christian propaganda

Almost as soon as the Battle of Kosovo was over, it was used in Christian propaganda. An account written in October 1389 describes how, as Jesus had twelve disciples, twelve knights fought their way through to the Sultan:

'Glorious, very glorious are the hands of the twelve knights who hacked their way through the enemy lines and circle of chained camels to reach Murat's tent. Most glorious of all is the knight who stabbed the Sultan dead with his sword.'

Albanians and Serbs in alliance

Historian Noel Malcolm writes that Kosovo's racial troubles have little root in history:

'There have been many battles and wars in Kosovo over the centuries, but until the last 100 years or so none of them had the character of an "ethnic" conflict between Albanians and Serbs. Members of those two populations fought together as allies at the battle of Kosovo in 1389 – indeed, they probably fought as allies of both sides of that battle ...' (*Kosovo A Short History*)

Murat I. Murat's forces seem to have won the Battle of Kosovo, but both he and Lazar were killed. After the battle the Turks continued their advance northwest through the Balkans, and in 1459 Serbia became a Turkish province.

Although the Serbs had been forced to retreat and their leader had been killed, the Battle of Kosovo came in time to be seen as a glorious moment in Serb history. (This is similar to the way in which some Americans came to admire General Custer's defeat at Little Big Horn in 1876, and some British took pride in their withdrawal at Dunkirk, 1940.) The story of the Battle of Kosovo was handed down from generation to generation in song and story. The facts were distorted and history was replaced by mythology. The idea of the 'Kosovo Covenant' entered Serb culture. It was said to be better to die fighting and to be rewarded in heaven than to live in slavery.

By the late 19th century, when Serbia was emerging as an independent state again, the mythology of the Battle of Kosovo helped build Serb nationalism. It gave the

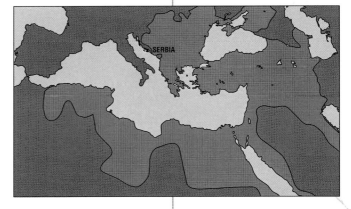

Turkish Sultan Osman I established the Ottoman Empire in 1301. Serbia became a province of the Empire in 1459. The yellow shading here shows the extent of the Ottoman Empire in the 17th century.

Serbs a pride in their past and hope for the future. In the 1990s, when Slobodan Milosevic decided to bring Kosovo more firmly under Serb control, his policy brought joy to many Serb hearts.

While Serbia (including Kosovo) was part of the Ottoman Turkish Empire, the Muslim Turks allowed the Christians some freedom of worship. For hundreds of years the headquarters (Patriarchate) of the Serbian Orthodox Church was at Pec, in Kosovo. After the collapse of the Ottoman Empire, the Serb Church's affection for Pec continued. From 1920 onwards, one of the titles of the head of the Serbian Church was 'Archbishop of Pec'. This is yet another reason why Serbs are deeply attached to Kosovo.

After numerous revolts and wars, in 1878 Serbia finally became an independent state again. However, large areas of the old medieval Serbia, including most of Kosovo, remained in Turkish hands. Therefore, although there was great rejoicing in Serbia, it was most unlikely that things would remain as they were for long.

Voislav Seselj at an anti-NATO protest in Belgrade, March 1999.

The Serb view in 1995

In 1995, as the war that broke up Yugoslavia was drawing to a close, some Kosovars were suggesting that Kosovo should be given independence as part of the peace settlement. Serbia's Deputy Prime Minister Voislav Seselj would have none of it:

'One thousand years ago, the cornerstone of Serb statehood, of its national consciousness and culture, was created in Kosova and Metohija ... One cannot imagine a Serb state without Kosova and Metohija.' (From an article in the *Greater Serbia Journal*, 14 October 1995)

KOSOVO AND YUGOSLAVIA, 1900-80

The decline of the Ottoman Empire encouraged ethnic groups to form their own independent states. By 1900 the Serbs, Romanians, Montenegrins and others had achieved this, but not yet the Albanians. In 1912, they launched a massive revolt against their Turkish overlords. It resulted in self-rule within the Ottoman Empire being granted both to Kosovo and to Albania.

Serbian soldiers during the 1913 Balkan War.

The Kosovars' new-found freedom did not last. Seeing Turkish weakness, in 1913 the Serbs joined with other Balkan states to attack the Ottoman Empire. They claimed they were 'liberators'. In reality, they were using the situation to grab more territory for themselves. The Serbs, of course, moved into Kosovo,

 Exaggeration

In 1905 a young Serbian diplomat Milan Radic complained that reports of attacks on Serbs in Kosovo were being exaggerated. He pointed out that between January and May 1905, for example, twenty-five Serbs were slain in Kosovo. Four were killed by other Serbs and another three by unknown killers.

'Is that number so desperately large? In Serbia many more people were killed in the same period ... And why is it that we ... categorically assert in our daily bulletins that there are one or two murders every single day, when we know perfectly well that there are only twenty-five in five months?' (quoted in Malcolm, *Kosovo A Short History*)

the land they had always regarded as theirs. Alarmed, many Kosovo Albanians joined the Turks to resist the invaders. They were swiftly swept aside, and by 22 October the Serbs were celebrating in Prishtina. At last, they declared, they had avenged their defeat at the Battle of Kosovo of 1389.

The Kosovo Albanians did not share Serb delight. Unlike their fellow Albanians to the south, who now had an independent Albania, the Kosovo Albanians had merely swapped one master – the Turk – for another – the Serb. The roots of the 1999 Kosovo crisis can be traced directly back to this dark moment in 1913. Dark it was. Serb soldiers, including paramilitary forces, saw the Albanians in Kosovo as aliens in a Serb land. They destroyed Albanian villages and massacred thousands of civilians. Serbs were urged to migrate to Kosovo and Albanians to emigrate. Thus the seeds of ethnic cleansing were sown.

The seeds of ethnic cleansing

The Carnegie Endowment for International Peace funded a commission to enquire and report on 'the causes and conduct of the Balkan Wars'. The report described the treatment of Kosovo's Albanians in 1912-13:

'Houses and whole villages reduced to ashes, unarmed and innocent populations massacred ... such were the means which were employed ... by the Serb-Montenegrin soldiery, with a view to the entire transformation of the ethnic character of regions inhabited exclusively by Albanians.' (Report of the International Commission, 1914)

The First World War

Fortunately for the Albanians, Serb rule was short-lived. On the outbreak of the First World War (1914), Serbia was invaded by its enemies, Austria-Hungary, backed by Bulgaria. By 1915 Serb resistance was broken, and Austria-Hungary and Bulgaria divided Kosovo between them.

The Serbian people

In 1914 Western Europe and the USA knew little of the Kosovo problem. They saw Serbia as a small, proud nation battling against the bullying Austro-Hungarian Empire. The first part of a history of the First World War, written at the time, described the Serbs:

'Sturdy, simple, industrious, and amazingly brave, the Serbian people have from the first revealed many admirable qualities ... The real Serbian, the man who has won war after war, is the peasant, the farmer, the countryman, who, ... living honestly and working hard, has helped to build up a great people.' (Wilson and Hammerton ed., *The Great War*, 1914)

(Right) Serb nationalist Gavrilo Princip is arrested after assassinating the heir to the Austrian throne, Franz Ferdinand, in Sarajevo, 28 June 1914. The assassination triggered the First World War, as Austria invaded Serbia and other European powers joined in.
(Above) Serbs test captured Austrian rifles, Belgrade, 1915.

In 1918, as French, Italian and Serbian forces swept through the Balkans, the wheel of fortune swung round yet again. When the war ended, Kosovo was once more under Serb control.

The creation of Yugoslavia

On 1 December 1918 a new Balkan super-state was proclaimed. The Kingdom of Serbs, Croats and Slovenes (renamed Yugoslavia in 1929) was made up of Serbia, Slovenia, Croatia, Bosnia-Herzegovina and Montenegro. Serbia dominated. Kosovo, occupied by the Serbs in 1912-13 but never taken over legally, was included in Yugoslavia as simply a part of Serbia. Some Kosovars – the Kacaks, or armed rebels – forcibly resisted the Serb occupation. Their efforts merely increased the Serbs' determination not to move.

From 1918 to 1939, the Serbs tried hard to make Kosovo genuinely Serbian. They used four tactics to obliterate Albanian culture. First, Serbo-Croat became the official language of government and education. Second, most key government jobs went to Serbs. Third, in the name of 'agrarian reform', Serbs were encouraged to move to Kosovo. Emigrants were even asked to return from the USA. Some 70,000 'colonists' arrived and were given land taken from Albanians. However, few Serbs felt at home in Kosovo, and the ratio of Serbs to Albanians did not rise much above 1:10.

A comparison with the Nazis

In 1937 a Serb historian Vaso Cubrilovic drew a direct parallel between the way the Nazis were behaving towards the Jews and the way the Serbs should treat the Kosovo Albanians.

'At a time when Germany can expel tens of thousands of Jews ... the shifting of a few hundred thousand Albanians will not lead to the outbreak of a world war.' (*The Expulsion of the Albanians by the Serbs*, quoted in Malcolm, *Kosovo A Short History*)

Not surprisingly, as life in Kosovo became harsher for Albanians, many emigrated. Perhaps as many as 150,000 left for Albania, Turkey and other countries. During the 1930s plans were also drawn up to drive out the remaining Kosovo Albanians by force. The tactics proposed were not unlike those used by Milosevic in the 1990s.

Belgrade, the capital of Yugoslavia, 1941: hanging was one of the many atrocities that the Nazi invaders committed against Serbs during the Second World War.

The Second World War

With the Second World War the situation changed yet again. In 1941 the Nazis overran Yugoslavia, and divided Kosovo among themselves, the Italians and the Bulgarians. The new masters were keen to get the locals on their side and so reversed the anti-Albanian policies. It was now the Serbs' turn to suffer racial discrimination, and thousands of colonists withdrew to Serbia. Thus the well of bitter memories on either side grew deeper still.

The headquarters of the Yugoslav Communist Party, Belgrade, 1963. A policeman stopped the photographer from taking any more pictures.

Communism

After the Second World War, Yugoslavia passed into Communist hands. Some Kosovars forcibly resisted the Communists until the 1950s, fearing that the new regime was just Serbian power in another form.

At first it looked as if they were right. The new Communist Yugoslavia consisted of six republics (Serbia, Bosnia-Herzegovina, Montenegro, Croatia, Slovenia and Macedonia). In theory, each looked after its own internal affairs. Kosovo's request to be a republic had been turned down. Instead, it was just a province.

The situation for the Kosovo Albanians was not as bad as during the 1930s. For example, some

Albanian-speaking schools were opened. Nevertheless, prominent Serbs in the all-powerful Communist Party maintained Serb influence in Kosovo. The Albanians' position was not helped when Yugoslavia, under President Tito, fell out with the USSR in 1948. Albania, also a Communist state, sided with the USSR. Albanians in Yugoslavia were then suspected of being enemies of the state.

Under President Tito, Yugoslavia was more open to outside influence than other Communist countries. Western newspapers were sold in Belgrade, and people could listen to US radio.

The houses of Kosovo Albanians were frequently searched. The people were arrested and questioned for little or no reason, and they found it even harder to get jobs. It is estimated that, by 1953, Serbs and Montenegrins made up 27 per cent of Kosovo's population but held 68 per cent of government and Communist Party positions in the province. Yet again, Albanians felt forced to emigrate. Perhaps 100,000 left for Turkey.

By the 1960s, Kosovo was an underfunded, neglected backwater of Yugoslavia. The low point came in 1963, when it was made an 'autonomous province' of Serbia. In reality, it was little more than one region of Serbia. Anti-Communist feeling ran high there.

The influence of President Tito

Kosovo's fortunes were restored by Marshal Tito, who was prime minister of Yugoslavia from 1945 to 1953 and president from 1953 to 1980. To hold his country together and keep himself in power as president, he had to balance the different ethnic groups against each other. In particular, he had to keep Serb ambition under control. Being part-Croat and part-Slovene himself, he understood the task well.

In 1967 Tito visited Kosovo and publicly criticized the treatment of its Albanians. The Serbs backed off. Kosovo gained greater independence, and in 1974 was given almost as much independence as the Yugoslav republics. The Serbs were not amused. Nor were they pleased when, in the late 1960s, Tito improved relations with Albania again. The Albanian flag could be flown in Kosovo, and an Albanian-speaking university was

Marshal Tito, seen here in 1967, improved conditions for Kosovo Albanians.

Events of 1968

In August 1968 the Russians invaded Czechoslovakia to quell a movement to liberalize the Communist government there. Tito feared that the Russians might next move against Yugoslavia. On 27 November 1968, Kosovo Albanian demonstrators took to the streets of Prishtina chanting:

'We want a university! Down with the colonial policy in Kosovo! Kosovo – a republic!'

Tito needed the support of all ethnic groups. So, although the demonstration was forcibly broken up, he did not crack down on the Kosovo Albanians but went some way to meeting their demands. The University of Prishtina was set up the following year.

Serbs driven out

The Serbs and Albanians each believed the other was in the wrong over Kosovo. This extract from an official history of the region on the Yugoslav government website, 1999, gives the Serb position:

'After 1968, many Serbian villages and many remaining Serbian homes in the Albanized settlements all over Kosovo and Metohija were finally emptied. The Albanians harvested wheat in Serbian estates, grabbed cattle, cut grass in the meadows, took away the harvested wheat, and beat to death or killed the victims, especially if they resisted.'

A Kosovo Albanian with the Albanian flag, 1998. The flag is a strong symbol of the fight for independence from Serbia.

established in Prishtina in 1969. Albanian staff were hired, students flooded in, and the university became a thriving centre of Albanian learning and culture. Albanians also took up positions of power in the Communist Party.

Population change

The Serbs were further alarmed by changes in Kosovo's ethnic balance. Feeling increasingly out of place, Serbs were leaving the province. Serbian sources say that they left to escape persecution. A more important reason for the population change was the birth rate. The Albanian birth rate had soared to the highest in Europe, while the Serb birth rate was falling. By 1981 the ratio of Albanians to Serbs in Kosovo had returned to approximately 10:1. The Serbs, a shrinking and threatened minority, were frightened. And, like many frightened people, they were ready to try desperate measures.

TENSION AND TERROR, 1981-95

The death of Tito

President Tito died in 1980. He had dominated Yugoslav politics since 1945, and his death was a major turning point in Yugoslavia's history. The weak system of government that replaced him might have worked in a prosperous, contented country, but during the 1980s Yugoslavia was neither prosperous nor content. Interest on foreign loans swallowed up 10 per cent of its income. Living standards were falling and unemployment was high. By the later 1980s inflation was soaring out of control.

Each of Yugoslavia's regions had its own culture, history and traditions, and the differences between the regions were often reinforced by linguistic differences. The country was held together by the Communist Party, the army, the police and a belief that, on balance, the republics were better off in Yugoslavia than outside. Under Tito's ruthless leadership, the forces maintaining Yugoslavia had the upper hand. After his death, the balance began to swing the other way. The change began in Kosovo.

These young Yugoslavs formed part of President Tito's guard in the late 1970s.

Discontent in Kosovo

Yugoslavia's economic problems were at their worst in Kosovo. The Communist government guaranteed everyone a job but, in fact, out of a population of some 1.5 million, perhaps 250,000 Kosovars were without work. Almost one third of the best-paid jobs in the province were held by Serbs and Montenegrins, who were, at most, 15 per cent of the population.

Kosovo's poverty was not inevitable. Its abundant natural resources (coal, iron and other minerals) could have made it very wealthy. But the mines, power plants and factories were badly run. Moreover, the Serbs insisted that most of Kosovo's industrial output had to be exported to Serbia at rock-bottom prices. Clearly, Tito's efforts to cut Serb control of Kosovo had met with only limited success.

Albanians attacked in Serbia

According to some Albanian reports, Serb attacks on Albanians were not limited to Kosovo:

'The first attacks of Serbia, that took the character of segregation and apartheid, were provoked on the shops of Albanians and individuals in Serbia in 1981. In Pozarevac, in Serbia, an Albanian child had his eyes taken out by civilian Serbs. Many physical attacks and ill-treatments were organized, by both Serbian individuals and state bodies ...' (The Institute of History, Prishtina, *Expulsions of Albanians and Colonization of Kosova*, 1997)

Discontent finally came into the open in the spring of 1981. Protest began among the students of Prishtina University and quickly moved into the streets. Over the next few weeks it spread to other towns and cities. Stone-throwing mobs clashed with the police, who replied with tear gas and baton charges. There were many casualties. The government said that ten people died; some locals reckoned – unrealistically – that the figure was nearer 1,000. Eventually, the Yugoslav army moved in with tanks, and a state of emergency was declared. Thousands of demonstrators were arrested and sent to prison.

Who were the demonstrators? Some were just hooligans making a nuisance of themselves. The majority were probably ordinary Kosovars complaining about such matters as low wages, unemployment, poor housing and dreadful conditions at work. But there were also those with more political interests – anti-Communists calling for democratic rights, and Kosovo nationalists. Some nationalists wanted Kosovo to have independence within Yugoslavia. Others sought complete independence. A few wanted union with Albania.

Not all Kosovo Albanians approved of the protests. For example, those who were part of the Communist leadership condemned the rioting as strongly as any Serb. Nevertheless, the evil stench of ethnic hatred hung in the air. Inevitably, Albanian thugs took advantage of the chaos to attack Serb homes, beating up the men and raping the women. Such incidents were probably few and far between, and not part of an organized campaign. An independent committee of Serbian human rights activists said that rape was a far more common crime inside Serbia proper than in Kosovo.

December 1988: fearing attack by Albanians, a Kosovo Serb mother carries a rifle with which to defend her family.

Nevertheless, in tense situations it is often not what actually happens that matters, but what people believe is happening. Fear spread among the Serb minority in Kosovo, and, throughout the 1980s, a steady stream left for Serbia proper. Serbian politicians and writers were quick to turn the situation to their advantage. This led to what historian Noel Malcolm has called a Serb-Albanian 'culture war'.

Against a background of economic decline and violence, writers on both sides made often unfounded claims and counter-claims. Albanians pointed to the long history of Serb repression in Kosovo. Serbs condemned

The value of information

Dobrica Cosic, a Serb nationalist politician, mounted an anti-Albanian propaganda campaign. He spread information such as a 'Memorandum' produced for him in 1985 by the Serbian Academy of Sciences claiming that Kosovo Serbs were being subjected to 'physical, political, judicial and cultural genocide'. A pro-Albanian website, *Kosovo Crisis Centre* (1999), quotes Cosic as explaining:

'Lying is a form of our patriotism and is evidence of our innate intelligence. We lie in a creative, imaginative, and inventive way.'

what they called the Albanian 'genocide' of Kosovo's Serbs since 1981, and said that over one quarter of a million Albanians had entered Kosovo illegally since 1940. Encouraged by such dubious information, the Serbs organized protest marches and petitions calling on the government in Belgrade (the capital of Serbia) to come to their rescue.

Slobodan Milosevic, 1988. Before entering politics full-time in 1984, he had studied law and worked in business administration. He had been the head of a gas company and president of a bank. As President of the League of Communists of Serbia, from late 1987, he demanded that the federal Yugoslav government should give Serbia full control over its provinces of Kosovo and Vojvodina.

Enter Milosevic

No one exploited the situation better than Serbia's Deputy Party President, Slobodan Milosevic. On 24 April 1987 Milosevic went reluctantly to Kosovo Polje in Kosovo to speak with Serbian nationalists. During the meeting in the House of Culture, pre-planned rioting broke out among a crowd of Serbs gathered

Attacks on the Serbs

Writing to the *New York Times* from Belgrade, reporter David Binder reported how the situation in Kosovo looked to him in November 1987:

'Ethnic Albanians in the Government have manipulated public funds and regulations to take over land belonging to Serbs ... Slavic Orthodox churches have been attacked, and flags have been torn down. Wells have been poisoned and crops burned. Slavic boys have been knifed ...'

outside. Milosevic came out onto the balcony and made a powerful off-the-cuff speech sympathizing with the mob's fears and demands. His delighted audience started chanting, 'Slobo! Slobo!' The scene was shown time and again on Serbian TV. Almost overnight, 'Slobo' became a Serbian national hero.

Milosevic quickly turned his popularity into power. Radio Television Belgrade gave him plenty of coverage, showing his actions and speeches in a favourable light. He organized carefully managed mass rallies, and got his followers into key positions in the Serbian

Belgrade, November 1988: Serbian nationalists support Milosevic's moves to abolish the autonomous status of Kosovo.

No interest in Kosovo

Before 1987 Slobodan Milosevic had shown little interest in the Kosovo situation. Indeed, as Deputy Party President, he once urged the Serbian Party President:

'Forget about the provinces, let's get back to Yugoslavia.' (Quoted in Malcolm, *Kosovo A Short History*)

Playing the Kosovo card

Slobodan Milosevic rose to power by 'playing the Kosovo card' – putting himself forward as the protector of Serbian interests in the region the Serbs regarded as theirs by right. He never lost an opportunity to remind people of Kosovo's importance, as in a speech in 1988:

'Every nation has a love which eternally warms its heart. For Serbia it is Kosovo.' (Quoted in Silber and Little, *The Death of Yugoslavia*)

government and Communist Party. By the end of 1987 he was President of the Serbian League of Communists and virtually dictator of Serbia.

Having built up his power in Serbia and Montenegro by getting his supporters into positions of influence, Milosevic was ready to move on Kosovo. In late 1988 he dismissed Kosovo Albanians from the Communist leadership, and this caused more protests to sweep across the province. But Milosevic was not put off. He prepared to change the constitution of Serbia to reduce Kosovo's independence. Yet again, Kosovo erupted. Faced with strikes, riots and marches, Serbia declared a state of emergency in Kosovo. The Yugoslav army moved in and hundreds of protestors were arrested.

Prishtina, November 1988: Kosovo Albanians protest against the dismissal of Albanians from the Communist leadership. They carry the Albanian and Yugoslav flags, and a picture of President Tito.

In March 1989 the Kosovo assembly (parliament) met to discuss the proposed new constitution. The assembly building was surrounded by tanks and armoured cars. Sinister-looking 'guests' (Serb police and security officers) mingled with the politicians. Not surprisingly, the new constitution was accepted. Kosovo had lost virtually all its independence. Serbia now controlled Kosovo's police, law courts and the social, economic and education departments of the government. Serbia could even decide what should be the official language of Kosovo.

Opposition

A fresh wave of protest was dealt with even more harshly than the last. There were many deaths and imprisonments. 25,000 extra police were sent into Kosovo, and many leaders of the Albanian community – lawyers, doctors, teachers and intellectuals – were imprisoned. Despite the repression, in December 1989, Kosovo intellectuals founded a moderate opposition party, the Democratic League of Kosovo (DLK). It was led by Dr Ibrahim Rugova, a writer-turned-politician whose father and grandfather had been killed by the Serbs in 1945. The League rejected violence and called on the outside world to put pressure on Yugoslavia to stop the Serb take-over of Kosovo.

 An interview with Rugova

Warren Zimmerman describes an interview he had in 1989 with Ibrahim Rugova (left):

'I asked him how the Albanians had treated Serbs when they had the upper hand before the Milosevic period. "Unfortunately," he answered without hesitation, "there were many crimes committed against Serbs."' (Quoted on Press Association website, 1999)

Although the League's pleas fell on deaf ears, its leaders continued their moderate programme. In July 1990 Albanian members of the Kosovo assembly, locked out of their building because of the state of emergency, met in the street and declared Kosovo to be an 'independent entity' within Yugoslavia. In 1991 a secret referendum (popular vote) was taken on whether Kosovo should be an entirely independent country. Apparently 99 per cent voted 'yes'. The next year, secret elections were held for a new assembly and government, headed by Rugova.

Serbianization

Whatever the result of these votes, Kosovo remained a police state. In March 1990 the Serbian government launched the Programme for the Realization of Peace and Prosperity in Kosovo. In June came a fresh series of emergency decrees. Both the Programme and the decrees were to hasten the Serbianization of Kosovo. Serbs were helped with government grants, housing and jobs. The official status of the Albanian language was removed. Its newspaper and educational institutions were closed. Albanians could not buy or sell property. Their teachers, doctors and civil servants were dismissed. The government offered to help Albanians only with birth control (to alter the province's ethnic balance) and emigration.

1990: Yugoslav tanks arrive in Podujevo, Kosovo, after clashes between Kosovo Albanians and police.

Victims

In 1990 thousands of Kosovo Albanian children suffered from a mysterious poisoning. The Albanians claimed it was the work of the Serbs, who were also destroying the Albanians' education system.

'In March 1990, Serbia organized poisoning of more than 7,000 Albanian school children and other children of pre-school age ...
In 1991 it closed all middle schools and a number of elementary schools and stopped financing education in the Albanian language, from kindergartens to university.' (The Institute of History, Prishtina, *Expulsions of Albanians and Colonization of Kosova*, 1997)

> ## Cultural importance
>
> In an official statement on its website in 1999, the Serb-dominated Yugoslav Ministry of Foreign Affairs explained the importance of Kosovo to Serb culture, although Serbs were a minority there:
>
> 'Archaeologists and art historians have identified and researched some 1300 monuments of the Serbian medieval culture in Kosovo and Metohija. According to the widespread opinion of experts, it is hard to find so many outstanding monuments of a national culture anywhere in the world.'

The Albanians were virtually aliens in their own land. Their reports told of arbitrary search and imprisonment, torture, eviction from homes and farms, assaults and rapes. The Albanians had certainly been guilty of crimes against Serbs in the early 1980s, but nothing they had done came close to the systematic persecution they now had to endure.

Yugoslavia begins to break up

Meanwhile the other Yugoslav republics had followed Milosevic's policies in Kosovo with increasing alarm. Slovenes, Croatians and Muslims feared that Milosevic's real aim was a Serb take-over of all Yugoslavia. In 1990 nationalist parties gained popularity at the expense of the Communists in all the Yugoslav republics apart from Serbia and Montenegro. The next year, Croatia and Slovenia declared their independence from Yugoslavia. Macedonia followed in September, and Bosnia in March 1992.

Many Serbs living outside Serbia wished to remain in a Serb-dominated Yugoslavia, and were prepared to fight to achieve this. As a result, Yugoslavia was not broken up by popular vote. It was torn apart by four years of brutal and fiendishly complicated civil war. Serbia's 'Kosovo problem' had become international.

Many Serbs were prepared to fight to try to prevent the break-up of Yugoslavia. This Bosnian Serb soldier is firing a machine gun near Srebrenica, in eastern Bosnia, July 1995.

BLOODBATH, 1992-98

(Right) A member of the Kosovo Liberation Army, masked and armed with a hunting rifle, March 1998.

Demanding independence

In 1992, inspired by events in Bosnia, Croatia, Slovenia and Macedonia, Rugova's DLK party demanded full independence for Kosovo. However, a small group of ethnic Albanian paramilitaries based in Macedonia believed that Rugova would never get what he wanted by peaceful means. Milosevic, they said, only understood force. So, in 1992, they formed the Kosovo Liberation Army (KLA). Its long-term aim was to join Kosovo, Albania and Macedonia in a single state.

The KLA used small bands of lightly armed but well-trained guerrillas. Numbering no more than about 500, it avoided open confrontation with the Yugoslav army. Instead, starting in 1995, it launched hit-and-run attacks on individuals, buildings and the police. These tactics gave Milosevic a useful propaganda weapon. He could now argue that his strong-arm measures in Kosovo were necessary to stamp out terrorism.

(Left) The father of this house in the Kosovan village of Malo Gracko was shot by an unknown attacker in November 1998. It was thought that the KLA shot him, for alleged loyalty to Serbia.

The war in Yugoslavia

The world's attention was diverted away from Kosovo for a time by the war in Yugoslavia. In 1992, US President George Bush warned Milosevic not to attack Kosovo, and international observers were sent there to report on human rights abuses. But when Milosevic expelled the observers the following year, the West protested but took no action. The only mention of Kosovo in the Dayton Accord that ended the war (1995) was that Serbia would not be fully recognized until it granted the region a degree of independence.

President Milosevic of Serbia, President Tudjman of Croatia and President Izetbegovic of Bosnia (seated, left to right) sign the Dayton Accord, December 1995.

A Western condition

After the end of the war in Yugoslavia, the USA and the EU put pressure on Serbia to restore Kosovo's rights and liberties. Malcolm Rifkind, British Foreign Secretary, explained in December 1996:

'Kosovo is a crucial element to peace in the Balkans and we have made it clear to Belgrade that there can be no return of access to international financial institutions, nor can there be a progressive relationship with the European Union, unless there is progress in Kosovo involving a return to autonomy.'

Ethnic cleansing

Serbia's Deputy Prime Minister Voislav Seselj wrote in the *Greater Serbia Journal* of 14 October 1995:

'There are around 400,000 ... foreigners in Yugoslavia today ... those who have been proven to be extremists will be immediately expelled, while others must possess the proper documents, the most important being the citizenship document [a kind of identity card], something none of them of course has.'

Srebrenica was one area of Bosnia where Serbs carried out ethnic cleansing.
Here, Muslim women and children commemorate the thousands of Muslim men who were massacred in the area in July 1995.

Bosnia saw the bitterest fighting of the war. The Serbs there were outnumbered by Muslims of various ethnic backgrounds. When the republic voted for independence from Yugoslavia in March 1992, the Bosnian Serbs, led by Radovan Karadzic, refused to accept this. Instead, Karadzic hoped to join Bosnia to a Greater Serbia. Until 1993 he was supported openly by Milosevic. The Bosnian Serbs aimed to conquer Bosnia and make it a largely Serb state. To achieve this, they introduced a policy that revolted the entire civilized world – 'ethnic cleansing'.

Ethnic cleansing meant getting rid of unwanted ethnic groups. It involved destroying settlements and driving out the inhabitants. Serb soldiers also raped women so they would bear Serb children. Non-Serb men were herded into concentration camps and held in appalling conditions. Most terrible of all, on occasion, men, women and children were simply slaughtered. Their bodies were burned or buried in mass graves. The ethnic cleansing in Bosnia was a frightful portent of what was to happen in Kosovo.

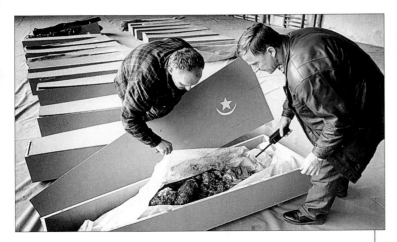

1996: Bosnian Muslims examine remains found in a mass grave and try to identify friends and relatives lost in the ethnic cleansing.

The early 1990s in Kosovo

The United Nations responded to Serbian atrocities by imposing sanctions on Yugoslavia (or 'Sloboslavia' as some Serbs jokingly called it) in May 1992. All trade with the country, now comprising only Serbia and Montenegro, was banned. This hit Kosovo badly, increasing poverty and unemployment. Many families survived only with the assistance of foreign aid workers.

At the same time, the Serbs tightened their grip on Kosovo. They spoke of Kosovo Albanians as 'guests' and replaced Albanian place-names with Serb ones. Fresh attempts were made to get Serbs to 'colonize' Kosovo. In 1991 the Belgrade government had offered free land (often taken from Albanians) to Serb immigrants. Later Serb refugees from former Yugoslavia, particularly Croatia, were resettled in Kosovo.

Humanitarian intentions?

'The Serbian regime brought about 500-700 new Serbian colonists to Kosova during the summer of 1995, settling them even by force in the ... property of Albanians. In spite of Serbian pompous propaganda that the action had a humanitarian character, it is clear that the main intention ... is to change the ethnic structure of the population and to colonize Kosova.' (Albanian Institute of History, 1997, quoted on *Kosova Information Centre* website)

Kosovo Albanians found the situation unbearable. By the end of 1993, perhaps half a million had fled abroad. If the Serbs hoped this exodus would alter the ethnic balance in Kosovo, however, they were mistaken. Few Serbs wished to live in the troubled region. There was always a steady flow of Serbs back into Serbia, and the colonization programme was a failure. By 1996, Kosovo was still largely an Albanian region. Yet, when Alexander Despic, the President of the Serbian Academy of Arts and Sciences, wondered out loud whether Serbia might let Kosovo go, he drew howls of protest. Serb nationalists said they would rather die than surrender their 'Jerusalem'.

Kosovo Serbs sell up

By early 1997, many Serbs in Kosovo felt their position had become hopeless. One official admitted:

'Many of us who have not yet sold up are preparing to do so now. We're the fools who didn't do so years ago. Now things are going in favour of the Albanians, prices are dropping. If we're not quick, they'll just grab [everything] from us for ever.' (Quoted in the *Daily Telegraph*, 16 February 1997)

Milosevic plays a double game

Milosevic was in a dilemma. He had come to power as a Serb nationalist. If he struck a deal with Rugova or the KLA, his support in Serbia would melt away. On the other hand, his Kosovo policy was costly and unsuccessful. It also angered the West, whose economic aid he desperately needed. (One Serb worker in ten was unemployed and inflation roared at 120 per cent a year.) Whatever Milosevic did, he seemed destined to lose.

So he played a double game. He allowed the persecution of the Albanians to continue. The KLA responded with more attacks, including shooting Serb traffic police in an ambush in Kosovo Mitrovica on 18

June 1996. Meanwhile, Milosevic met with Rugova in August and promised to lift the ban on schooling in the Albanian language in certain areas. Nothing happened, and the agreement only made Rugova appear weak. Nevertheless, the United Nations believed that Serbia was taking a softer line at last and so, in October, it lifted its economic sanctions.

In early 1997, Belgrade was full of people protesting that Milosevic should accept the results of local elections from November 1996. Below, left to right: opposition leaders Zoran Djindjic, Vesna Pesic and Vuk Draskovic. Eventually Milosevic admitted their majority in Belgrade's council. Djindjic became mayor of the city.

Despite this, by early 1997, Milosevic's position was looking even more uncertain. His Serbian Socialist Party (SPS) had been defeated in local elections. His refusal to recognize this led to violent anti-government protests in Belgrade. The USA was pressuring him to accept democracy and grant Kosovo home rule. The situation in Kosovo was

deteriorating, too. After the Serb rector of Prishtina University had been blown up by a car bomb in January, Kosovo Serbs feared for their lives. Some believed that Milosevic was about to abandon them.

A KLA statement

The Kosovo Liberation Army's Political Declarations are published on the KLA's website. Declaration number 8 is:

'The Liberation Army of Kosova ... entered [this war] with the motto: Kosova will be ours, or it will be ashes and dust, with the conviction that more honourable it is to die in the quest for freedom than to live under subjugation.'

A Serb policeman crouches by a wrecked car. The three people in it – workers at a Kosovo coal mine, coming from Belgrade – were shot, allegedly by the KLA.

The KLA's campaign grows

In the spring of 1997 the situation in Kosovo was changed by events in Albania. There, a sudden collapse of dubious get-rich-quick financial schemes destroyed many people's savings. In their fury they blamed the government. As the country descended into lawlessness, army barracks were looted and thousands of weapons stolen. Some of these found their way to the KLA.

Whether wielding stolen Albanian arms or not, the KLA's campaign grew in intensity. On 13 September 1997, using automatic rifles and grenades, they attacked ten Serb police stations in southern Kosovo at the same time.

Serb reports

This official statement appeared on the Yugoslav government website in 1999:

'Terrorism in Kosovo and Metohija escalated in its worst form during 1998. In the time between January 1st and October 31st, 1998, the Albanian terrorists committed ... a total of 1,496 terrorist attacks, out of which 624 or 41.7 per cent [were] against citizens and other facilities. During these attacks, 152 citizens were killed ...'

Relations between the KLA and Rugova's DLK had never been easy. Rugova wanted passive resistance, not violence, and he was prepared to talk with Milosevic. He had also said that he would accept self-government for Kosovo rather than full independence. The KLA was committed to fighting for a free Kosovo, and spoke of a single state for all Albanian peoples. By late 1997, several villages and towns in southern Kosovo were under its control.

The Serb response

Rugova knew the Serb dictator well enough to realize that he would not accept this situation for long. Fearing a 'bloodbath', in December 1997 he begged the USA and the European Union (EU) to mediate in Kosovo. The Serbs said no one had a right to interfere in their internal affairs. The West, unable to agree what to do, did nothing. As Rugova had predicted, the result was a bloodbath.

Early in 1998, the Serbian government in Belgrade cut all trade links with Kosovo and sent in heavily armed police and paramilitaries to tackle the KLA. Among the Serb forces were the dreaded Serbian Volunteer Guard, or 'Tigers', commanded by 'Arkan' (Zeljko Raznjatovic). The Tigers were a band of murderers armed with anything from butchers' knives to rifles. They drew no distinction between fighting the KLA and ethnic cleansing.

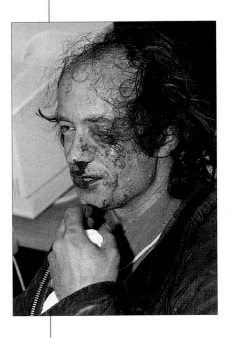

Television news camera-man Chris Wenner was beaten by Serb plain-clothed police as he filmed demonstrations in Prishtina, in April 1998.

Reports of horrific massacres of innocent citizens soon followed, first from the Drenica region, then from further afield. Villages were burned, and men, women and children were slaughtered. Huge crowds took to Prishtina's streets to protest. The police dispersed them with tear gas and bullets. When Milosevic sent a Yugoslav government delegation from Belgrade to Prishtina to talk, the Albanian leaders said the move was mere propaganda and refused to meet them.

Victims of the Serb paramilitaries

During the spring of 1998 Serb paramilitaries were operating in the Likoshan region of Kosovo. Among their victims were eleven people of the Ahmeti family. *Koha Ditore*, an Albanian daily paper published in Prishtina, reported on 1 March 1998:

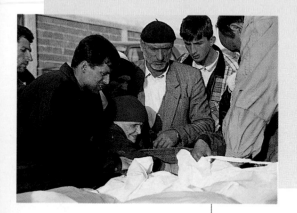

'Five or six big blood stains, broken teeth, brains all over the place, a piece of human jaw hanging down from the bushes, bullets of different calibres, are seen at the "scene of the crime" ... The police slaughtered them to death using shotguns and other hard and sharp objects.'

Dinore Ahmeti identifies the bodies of three of her sons.

Escalation

As the weather improved, the Serbs moved in tanks and artillery. The KLA, now consisting of several thousand men, fought back. The catalogue of atrocities committed by both sides mounted, and, by the late spring, 300,000 Kosovars were homeless refugees. Threatened with fresh international sanctions, in late March 1998 Milosevic promised to pull back his forces. No withdrawals were made.

By July the fighting in Kosovo was looking like full-blown war. The KLA was no longer just a guerrilla force. KLA fighters had captured almost 40 per cent of Kosovo and were defending their positions in battle. To many Kosovo Albanians Rugova's pacifism now looked irrelevant, and proposed talks with Serb leaders in May came to nothing.

The fight, however, was an unequal one. By August the KLA was retreating before Serb armour and aircraft. KLA strongholds were recaptured one by one. The advancing Serbs burned, tortured and looted, adding to the reports of atrocities coming from the war-torn

An attack on a KLA family

The international organization Human Rights Watch reported in 1998:

'A focal point of police attention [in the Drenica region] ... was the village of Donji Prekaz, and especially the family compound of Adem Jashari ... a local KLA leader. In ... March 1998, the police mounted attacks on the compound ... Jashari's entire family, save an eleven-year-old girl, was killed in the attack. Of fifty-eight bodies later buried, eighteen were women and ten were children sixteen years old or younger.'

region. The West was now seriously worried. What if the Serbs pursued the KLA into Albania, bringing that country into the war? Then Macedonia, Greece and even Turkey might become involved. And what would Russia, traditionally an ally of Serbia, do?

The Jashari house was pulled apart in the police attack.

Faced with the prospect of a full-scale international war, in September 1998 the United Nations demanded that both sides stop fighting. NATO prepared to enforce this demand with bombing raids. Finally, only hours before NATO launched air strikes, the US Special Envoy Richard Holbrooke persuaded Milosevic to call off his offensive. As the guns fell silent, the world waited to see what would happen next.

Milosevic is warned

In late September 1998, the defence ministers of NATO's member countries met at Vilamoura, Portugal, and warned Milosevic that they would launch air strikes if he did not comply with their demand that he should

'... take immediate steps to alleviate the humanitarian situation ... [and] stop repressive actions against the population and seek a political solution through negotiations with the Albanian majority.' (Quoted in the *Daily Telegraph*, 25 September 1998)

THE POWER OF NATO, 1998-99

Fragile agreement

In October 1998, Milosevic agreed to withdraw his forces to their positions of February 1998. He also said he would let aid agencies work in Kosovo, help refugees return home, co-operate with the International War Crimes Tribunal, and discuss Kosovo's future with the Albanians. International observers were to see that the ceasefire was kept.

Tragically, but understandably, the agreement did not last. The Albanians were divided. Ibrahim Rugova had lost popularity to the KLA. Some saw his willingness to compromise as a sign of weakness. The KLA itself was split. The one-time student activist Hashim Thaci, who reorganized the KLA after its defeats in 1998, rejected all compromise. The KLA's political leader, Adem Demaci, took a more moderate line.

Neither the KLA nor President Milosevic could afford to back down. The KLA existed only to make Kosovo independent of Serbia, while Milosevic's political future depended on his keeping Kosovo. He also needed Kosovo's wealth. In 1988 he had signed a $519 billion contract with a Greek mining company to

The importance of the mines

Novak Bjelic, director of Kosovo's state-owned Trepca mines, explained:

'The war in Kosova is about the mines, nothing else. This is Serbia's Kuwait – the heart of Kosova. We export to France, Switzerland, Greece, Sweden, the Czech Republic, Russia and Belgium ... We [also] export to a firm in New York ... Naturally, the Albanians want all this for themselves.' (Chris Hedges, *New York Times*, quoted on the *Kosova Crisis Centre* website, 1999)

exploit the Trepca mines. To maintain uninterrupted production, he had replaced most Albanian mine-workers with Serbs and Eastern Europeans. If he gave up Kosovo, he would lose the mines – a devastating blow to the Serbian economy.

Finally, too much blood had been spilt and too much hatred aroused for either side to trust the other. So when, between October and December 1998, US envoy Christopher Hill tried to get Serb and Albanian leaders into discussions, he made little progress. And as the weeks passed, the ceasefire looked increasingly shaky. In November, Albanian guerrillas shot two Serb policemen. The following month, Serb troops killed 36 KLA rebels and six Serbs died in a guerrilla attack on a café.

Premonitions of war

By Christmas 1998 the feeling among the Kosovo Albanians was that the ceasefire could not last. On 26 December one woman told a BBC reporter:

'We were thinking – hoping – it would be peace. But it is all changing now. So much shooting. We know it will be war again soon. We are accepting that.'

In January 1999 the crisis deepened. Over 40 unarmed Kosovo Albanians were found dead near Racak. Serb forces killed another 24 Albanians in a raid on a KLA hideout. By now the ceasefire had clearly broken down.

The bodies of villagers from Racak were found in a ditch on a nearby hill.

On 30 January a six-nation Contact Group (the USA, Britain, France, Italy, Germany and Russia) told both sides to attend peace talks. A settlement deadline was set for 20 February. NATO backed the efforts of the Contact Group by threatening to bomb those who refused to co-operate.

Peace talks

On 6 February the Contact Group met Serb government officials and Kosovo Albanians at the Château de Rambouillet, near Paris. The negotiations were extremely difficult. Russia was not a member of NATO and was unwilling to see that organization play a major part in resolving the conflict. As a result, it disagreed with the rest of the Contact Group over NATO's threat to bomb and the plan to send NATO peacekeepers into Kosovo. The Serbs also rejected the idea of foreign peacekeepers. The Albanians were split between the KLA members, led by Hashim Thaci, and the moderate Ibrahim Rugova and his supporters.

As the discussions dragged on, Serb soldiers and heavy weapons poured into Kosovo. NATO built up its own forces in the region, particularly US bomber aircraft.

Danish F-16 fighter planes at an Italian air base, ready to take part in the NATO action. It would be the first time ever that the Royal Danish Air Force had flown its fighters in combat.

This time, NATO leaders warned, they were in earnest. If no peace deal was struck, they really would attack.

In hope of an agreement, the 20 February deadline was extended by three days. The talks were then postponed until mid-March. In the meantime, the military build-up went on. By now the Serbs had six times more forces in Kosovo than permitted by the ceasefire agreement. More alarming, they were starting to use them. As the talks resumed on 15 March, the Serbs began a massive offensive against the KLA. Villages and farms were attacked, and once again Kosovo's roads were clogged with refugees.

Before the talks re-opened, the Albanians united to form a temporary KLA-led government for Kosovo. On 16 March this government accepted a set of peace proposals: self-rule for Kosovo within Yugoslavia, 28,000 NATO-led peacekeeping troops in Kosovo, withdrawal of Serb forces and surrender of KLA weapons. But these terms were unacceptable to Milosevic, and on 19 March the talks finally broke down. Three days later, US envoy Richard Holbrooke flew to Belgrade for last-minute discussions. Yet again, Milosevic refused to give way.

Belgrade, 22 March 1999: US envoy Richard Holbrooke (centre) and US mediator and ambassador to Macedonia, Christopher Hill (left), meet with Milosevic in a final attempt to reach agreement without war.

An unwanted result

Opponents of Milosevic's dictatorship believed that the NATO attacks would unite the Serbs behind their president and make the task of replacing him with a democratic form of government even more difficult. Vojin Dimitrijevic, director of the Centre for Human Rights in Belgrade, said:

'In one night ... the NATO airstrikes have wiped out 10 years of hard work of the ... democratic opposition.' (Quoted in *Newsweek*, 12 April 1999)

NATO goes to war

Nineteen NATO countries went to war with Serbia on 24 March 1999, the first time the alliance had waged war in Europe. Although their forces were overwhelmingly superior, they had insufficient troops and heavy weapons in the region to tackle the Serb army (114,000 soldiers, 1,400 heavy guns and 1,270 tanks) on the ground. Besides, such an invasion would have meant heavy losses that could have undermined public support for the campaign.

A car factory damaged by NATO bombing, April 1999.

Therefore, NATO decided on an air war. It targeted the Serb army and airforce, communications (including roads, bridges, power plants and TV stations), munitions dumps, supplies, command centres, and any other building or plant that enabled Serbia to wage war, even factories making everyday household goods. When the war began, NATO had almost 1,000 aircraft (ranging from B-52 heavy bombers to reconnaissance aircraft) and over 25 ships off the Balkan coast. Many of these vessels, including three nuclear submarines, were armed with sea-to-ground cruise missiles.

Kosovo Albanians saw NATO as their ally. (UCK are the Albanian initials for KLA.) When the war ended and NATO troops entered Kosovo, they were greeted as heroes.

For 78 days NATO bombs and missiles rained down mercilessly on Kosovo and Serbia. Troops were killed, armour destroyed, munitions blown up, bridges smashed, factories burned out, power stations put out of action. For a time Milosevic remained defiant. But as his country fell apart around him, he began to waver. On 10 May he said he was withdrawing his forces from Kosovo. NATO said that was not enough and carried on bombing. Three weeks later Milosevic

Betrayed

When NATO, led by the USA, began bombing Serbia, many ordinary Serbs felt they had been betrayed by the Americans. US shops and fast-food outlets in Belgrade were attacked. A Serbian historian explained that his people had seen the Americans as friends:

'We were more often on good terms with America than Russia. We really liked the Americans, and it's hard to forget that.' (Quoted in the *Times*, 1 April 1999)

Conflict on the Albanian side

During the war, Ibrahim Rugova was seen on TV trying to negotiate a peace deal with Milosevic. The KLA was reported to be furious.

'The KLA ... has condemned the moderate leader of the province's ethnic Albanians Dr Ibrahim Rugova to death ... the KLA is trying to remove Dr Rugova from the political scene since it does not agree with his efforts to reach a peaceful and political resolution to Kosovo's issue.' (Macedonian Press Agency, 27 April 1999)

began serious negotiations with Russian and EU diplomats. The bombing went on.

On 3 June the Serb parliament accepted a peace deal. The NATO air campaign did not stop. Two days later, NATO and Serb commanders began

The peace deal set a deadline of 15 June by which all Serb troops had to be withdrawn from Kosovo. This Serbian tank crew make the three-finger salute as they leave Drenica.

Why divide?

In an e-mail to an American friend, an ethnic Albanian girl living in Kosovo expressed her view:

'You mention the independence of Kosovo. I don't really give such an importance to the status. I don't see this as a war for getting divided ... Albanians and Serbs ... While Europe is trying to take the borders off ... we do not need to bring new ones.' (January 1999)

Milosevic in defeat

Even on the day of his defeat, Milosevic tried to sound upbeat:

'We have defended the only multi-ethnic society left over as a remnant of the former Yugoslavia. This is another great achievement.'
(11 June 1999)

face-to-face discussions. The Serbs, backed by the Russians, objected to NATO forces entering Kosovo if the Serbs withdrew. Still no let-up in the bombing. On 8 June the UN Security Council suggested a Kosovo peacekeeping force 'with NATO at its core'. The Serbs finally agreed to this.

NATO commander General Sir Mike Jackson and several Serb generals, including Colonel General Svetozar Marjanovic, signed a peace deal the following evening. The next day, when it was clear that Serb forces were pulling back, NATO stopped its bombing.

21 June 1999: General Sir Mike Jackson (left) and KLA chief Hashim Thaci sign an agreement on the demilitarization of the KLA.

A Serb Church view

In June 1999, the Serbs celebrated the 610th anniversary of the Battle of Kosovo with sadness in their hearts. Father Sava of the Decani monastery in Kosovo felt humiliated by the Serbs' defeat by NATO and blamed Milosevic for his people's troubles.

'This is not a defeat for our church, not for us. It is a defeat for Milosevic ... For us and our people it is a tragedy. The people are the victims ... It is we who have to suffer the evils he [Milosevic] produced.' (Quoted in the *Guardian*, 29 June 1999)

The Serbian media

The Serbian media heralded the peace agreement as victory. Bojan Cvetic of Belgrade was not impressed. He wanted food, not words:

'I'm fed up with the Serbian media. Victory, they say. What victory? Even if it was a victory you couldn't eat it.' (Quoted in the *Independent*, 12 June 1999)

The Serbs built dummy tanks, roads and bridges, to confuse the NATO bombers.

The war damage

Serbia had suffered massive damage. Forty-five bridges had been downed, no oil refineries were working, and dozens of factories and other plant had been destroyed. Perhaps 1,500 civilians had been killed. Nevertheless, although many Serbs had no jobs, their country still functioned. NATO estimated that 10,000 Serb soldiers had been killed and wounded. Yet the army withdrew from Kosovo in good order. Many of the 120 Serb tanks that NATO had hit turned out to have been dummies, and some sources said the true figure of tanks destroyed was as low as 20. Indeed, there were rumours that Milosevic had not surrendered because of the bombing but because Russia had threatened to cut Serbia's supplies of natural gas. (Russia may have done this because it was desperate for Western economic aid.)

The latest technology allowed NATO to bomb with great precision. Considering the thousands of missions flown, the number of civilian casualties (which NATO called 'collateral damage') was low. Nevertheless, there were dreadful mistakes. On 14 April, US planes attacked a slow-moving column of people and vehicles on a road near Meja, near the Albanian border. Sixty-four people were killed and many vehicles destroyed. Too late, NATO realized that it had bombed the people it was supposedly protecting – Albanian refugees crowded on to farm tractors, trailers and carts.

Seoul, South Korea, 13 May 1999: Chinese students protest against NATO's bombing of the Chinese embassy in Belgrade.

On 7 May, NATO bombs hit the Chinese embassy in Belgrade, killing three embassy staff. And on 1 June NATO warplanes accidentally bombed positions inside Albania.

NATO mistakes

The NATO-Serbia war was the first to be backed up by a propaganda war on the internet. Reports of NATO's mistakes were posted on the Yugoslav government site. For example:

'17 civilians were killed, and 43 severely wounded in a bombing of the bus near the place called Savine Vode on the road Pec-Rozaje. This is the seventh case of mass killing of the innocent civilians that the officials of NATO alliance ... call a "mistake".'

Refugees try to persuade Macedonian soldiers to let them leave a camp on the border of Kosovo and Macedonia, to get to a safer camp further inside Macedonia.

Refugees

The Serbs had started ethnic cleansing in Kosovo before NATO attacked. When the bombing started, the pace and ferocity of the operation increased dramatically. By the end of March, perhaps 100,000 people had been driven from their homes and were making their way towards the Albanian, Montenegrin

Refugees tell their stories

Interviewed in a Macedonian refugee camp, Dr Enver Alidema, a Kosovo Albanian, remembered vividly the night his family were 'ethnically cleansed':

'I feel very emotional talking about this ... Sometimes I was jealous of the dead. Our Serb neighbours knew what was going to happen and the soldiers were drunk, shooting in the air and beating people. "Where are your young women? Where is your gold? Where are your young men?" they were saying.' (From an interview with Bjorg Palsdottir of the neutral International Rescue Committee, 16 May 1999)

Another refugee from Albania reported:

'We were lined up against the wall and the police handed out clubs and metal bars to young Serbs to beat us. Some of the boys had to stand on cases of beer to reach the taller guys.' (Quoted in the *Independent*, 9 June 1999)

and Macedonian borders. Later, almost 20,000 refugees a day were leaving Kosovo. Many had lost everything. Serbs had destroyed their homes, looted their goods and confiscated their papers. Families had been split up. Large numbers of men had simply disappeared. By the end of the war, an estimated 900,000 Kosovars had left their homeland. Thousands of others had fled to the mountains and forests.

Keeping clean at a NATO refugee camp in Stenkovic, Macedonia.

The refugees – shocked, malnourished and often sick – were housed in hastily erected camps that soon swelled into tent cities. Thousands were taken abroad, to neighbouring countries, Western Europe and the USA. Many told appalling stories of Serb brutality: execution without trial, beatings, torture, rape and even mass murder. Because Serbia had not allowed the world's media to cover the events in Kosovo as they wished, concrete evidence was hard to find. But there were enough facts to show that the campaign against the Kosovo Albanians had been deliberate and brutal. On the strength of these findings, on 27 May the International War Crimes Tribunal charged Milosevic and four of his colleagues with 'crimes against humanity'.

Refugees on a reserve list for a flight to the UK wait to see if they will be leaving the camp.

WHAT NEXT?

As NATO troops entered Kosovo in June 1999, many Serb families left the region, fearing attacks by returning Albanians.

The peace of 10 June 1999 had been worked out by Finnish and Russian diplomats. It ended the bombing and Serbia's dreadful ethnic cleansing. As agreed, all Serb forces withdrew from Kosovo in an orderly manner, and a NATO-led United Nations peacekeeping force (KFOR) of around 50,000 troops moved in to maintain law and order. Unexpectedly, a small number of Russian troops also entered Kosovo and based themselves at Prishtina airport. The Russian authorities said this was a 'mistake'. In reality, it was Russia's way of making sure that NATO did not get everything its own way.

As soon as the peace agreement had been signed, it was clear the war had solved none of Kosovo's long-term problems. Milosevic, an indicted war criminal, was still in power. The majority of Serbs still regarded Kosovo as part of Serbia. Once the refugees had returned, the great bulk of Kosovo's population was still Albanian. Indeed, many Serbs left the province alongside their armed forces, making the Albanian

Milosevic rallies his people

On 10 June, after agreeing to withdraw his forces from Kosovo, President Milosevic gave a rallying TV speech to the Serbian people:

'Dear citizens. Happy peace to us all! ... We never gave up Kosovo ... We have shown that our army is invincible ... I wish all citizens of Yugoslavia much joy and success in the reconstruction of our country!'

The US achievement

US warplanes made up the bulk of the NATO strike force. On 10 June 1999 US President Bill Clinton spoke of his nation's achievement on behalf of the ethnic Albanians:

'Their only hope was that the world would not turn away in the face of ethnic cleansing and killing, that the world would take a stand. We did for 78 days. Because we did, the Kosovars will go home.'

majority even larger. A significant number of KLA officials still wanted an independent Kosovo or even union with Albania and Macedonia.

Furthermore, the war had created fresh difficulties. In time, international observers uncovered more and more evidence of Serbian cruelty and mass murder. Two torture chambers were found in Prishtina, for example. Mass rapes of Albanian women were said to have taken place at Dragacin on 5 April. On 20 June, KFOR found 60,000 refugees assembled in makeshift concentration camps based in burned-out villages near Podujevo. Most ghastly of all, dozens of mass graves, some

July 1999: a French KFOR soldier begins exhuming bodies from one of the mass graves.

Good and evil

British Prime Minister Tony Blair's statement on 10 June 1999 expressed the belief that the Kosovo peace deal was a victory of right over wrong.

'Good has triumphed over evil. Justice has overcome barbarism. And the values of the civilized world have prevailed.'

A mass grave

Serbs apparently tried to get rid of the evidence of their killings. A NATO spokesman who had examined a mass grave of 81 civilians near the town of Kacanik told the world's press on 14 June 1999:

' ... the injuries will show that they died by small-arms fire. But it is just as well we got here before they [the Serbs] finished, because we believe they were using a type of powder that would turn bodies to mush very quickly.'

containing hundreds of bodies, were reported in such places as Cirez, Dobrosevac, Nevoljane, Nakarad, Slovinje and Malisevo.

The horrors of ethnic cleansing had fuelled Albanian hatred of the Serbs. This posed real problems for the peacekeepers. During the war, the KLA had fought the Serbs on the ground under cover of NATO aircraft. Now, as their enemy withdrew, the KLA swept into Kosovo. Some KLA soldiers joined with angry mobs of Albanian civilians seeking revenge. The Kosovo Serbs huddled indoors, fearing they might now be ethnically cleansed by the Albanians. On occasion, KFOR soldiers shot Albanians who seemed to be threatening the peace. Elsewhere, KFOR soldiers were killed as they tried to clear Kosovo of mines and unexploded NATO bombs. They also struggled to protect Kosovo's ethnic gypsy population. Albanians claimed that the gypsies had sided with Serbia during the war.

July 1999: Albanians walk past a fire at a Serb-owned business in Gnjillane, Kosovo. Speaking of such revenge attacks, Albanians claimed that only buildings owned by Serbs responsible for war crimes were being burned.

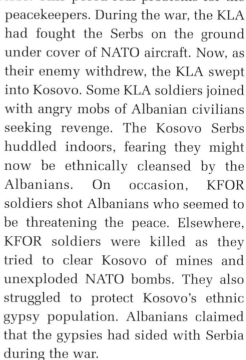

Post-war violence

Despite the presence of KFOR troops, Kosovo was still wracked by violence after the war. The Serbian Ministry of Information reported on 28 June 1999:

'Members of "KLA" are terrorizing non-Albanian population ... Fourteen civilians were killed on Thursday in the zone of responsibility of British troops ... Several Gypsy houses in Prishtina were set alight and about 60 people expelled ... Serb women, who had come to sell cheese, were chased away from the green market in a settlement of Prishtina.'

How was Kosovo to be governed?

The Rambouillet talks had planned for Kosovo to be given self-rule within Yugoslavia. But the ceasefire agreement of 10 June side-stepped the self-rule question. Immediately after the war the United Nations took over the running of the province. The UN Interim Administration Mission in Kosovo (UNMIK) was supported by other international organizations and promised massive aid from the European Union. Its first task was to resettle the refugees, who flooded back into Kosovo far more quickly than had been expected. It was a gigantic task. By mid-July the UN feared that hundreds of thousands of Kosovars would still be homeless by the time the winter snows began.

27 June 1999: like many Albanian shop- and restaurant-owners, Mustafa Djulderan removes the Serbo-Croat signs from the façade of his restaurant in Prishtina.

Little progress was made towards finding a permanent government for Kosovo. Belgrade continued to regard Kosovo as a province of Serbia. This was unacceptable to most KLA leaders. Even more disturbing, as the KLA had not been disarmed, some NATO sources feared civil war between the different KLA factions. These were led by Hashim Thaci, Ibrahim Rugova and Rexhep Qosja (an extremist leader who had refused to attend the Rambouillet talks).

Financing the KLA

Professor Michel Chossudovsky of the University of Ottawa, Canada, was clear where he thought the KLA got its money from:

'... the KLA is sustained by organized crime with the tacit approval of the United States and its allies ... [Moreover] the links of the ... KLA to criminal syndicates in Albania, Turkey and the European Union have been known to Western governments and intelligence agencies since the mid-1990s.' ('Kosovo "Freedom Fighters" Financed by Organized Crime', World Socialist Website, 10 April 1999)

(Below) A handbill from an anti-Milosevic demonstration in Belgrade, August 1999. The words say 'Never again – neither red nor black' (i.e. neither Communist nor Nazi).

(Opposite) 16 June 1999: refugees pour back from Albania to Kosovo, despite the threat of landmines left behind by Serb forces.

All three KLA groups had powerful backers supplying money from abroad. Albanians had for some time been prominent in Europe's illegal but highly profitable drug-smuggling trade. By the summer of 1999 the chances of Kosovo returning to peaceful democratic rule did not look good. Some feared that the KLA might end up dividing the area into hostile mini-states.

The outlook for Serbia

The outlook for Serbia was uncertain, too. The West wanted Milosevic replaced by a democratically elected government. However, despite his defeat and the destruction suffered by his country, he remained in power. Fed by unemployment and poverty, opposition protests mounted during July. But as long as the police and the army remained loyal, there was no chance of Milosevic going. Certainly, he had no intention of stepping aside voluntarily. And if he were pushed out, there was no guarantee that a democrat would take his place.

Sadly, after all the bloodshed, cruelty and good intentions, there seemed only one certainty about the Serbia-Kosovo problem. It would continue to break hearts and bodies in the new millennium as tragically as it had in the last.

DATE LIST

1389	Ottoman army defeats Serbian army at the Battle of Kosovo.	**1981**	Anti-government demonstrations in Kosovo. Rising ethnic tension leads to increasing Serb emigration.
1912	Albanian revolt against Turkish rule leads to establishment of Albania.	**1987**	Slobodan Milosevic comes to power in Serbia. He encourages Serbian nationalism.
1913	Serbs occupy Kosovo.	**1989**	Milosevic tightens Serbia's grip on Kosovo, using Yugoslav army and police to keep order.
1918	End of First World War. Kosovo is in the Kingdom of Serbs, Croats and Slovenes (later known as Yugoslavia), as part of Serbia.		Democratic League of Kosovo (DLK) is founded, with Ibrahim Rugova at its head.
1920s and 1930s	Serbia attempts to colonize Kosovo.	**1990**	Kosovo parliament shut down.
1941	Germany invades Yugoslavia. Kosovo is divided among Germany, Italy and Bulgaria.	**1991-95**	Civil war results in Croatia, Slovenia and Macedonia leaving Yugoslavia.
1945	End of Second World War. Kosovo, again part of Serbia, is in the Communist republic of Yugoslavia.	**1991**	Kosovo Albanians vote in secret for Kosovo to become an independent republic.
1963	Kosovo becomes 'autonomous province' of Serbia.	**1992**	Rugova is elected President of Kosovo in a secret vote.
1974	Revised constitution of Yugoslavia gives Kosovo more independence. Albanian majority's rights are recognized.		Kosovo Liberation Army (KLA) is established in Macedonia. Milosevic becomes President of Yugoslavia.
1980	Death of President Tito. Serbia begins attempt to clamp down on Kosovo Albanians.		Serbs begin ethnic cleansing in Bosnia. US President George Bush warns Serbs not to attack Kosovo.

1995	Dayton Peace Accord ends war in Yugoslavia (now consisting of Serbia and Montenegro only) but fails to settle the Kosovo problem.	**1999, January**	Slaughter of 45 Albanians outside Racak. West demands that Serbia and Kosovo Albanians attend peace talks or face air attack.
1996	KLA begins attacks on Serb officials in Kosovo. Talks between Milosevic and Rugova.	**February**	Peace talks at Rambouillet fail to reach agreement.
1997	KLA steps up its attacks.	**March**	Peace talks resume in Paris. Albanians accept a settlement. When Serbs refuse to accept NATO peacekeepers in Kosovo, talks break up. NATO launches air attacks on Serbia and on Serb forces in Kosovo. Serbia steps up its ethnic cleansing of Kosovo. Albanian refugees stream into Albania, Montenegro and Macedonia.
1998, January	Serbia launches attack on KLA. Ethnic cleansing in Kosovo.		
March	Serbian army enters Kosovo in force. Ethnic cleansing escalates. Many Albanians leave Kosovo.		
May	Milosevic and Rugova fail to reach agreement over crisis.	**April**	NATO steps up bombing. Number of refugees rises.
July	KLA controls 40 per cent of Kosovo before being driven back by Serb offensive.	**May**	Milosevic says he is withdrawing forces from Kosovo. United Nations calls for trial of Milosevic and four other Serb officials as war criminals.
September	Ethnic cleansing more violent. UN Security Council calls for immediate ceasefire in Kosovo.		
October	NATO threatens air strikes against Serbia. Milosevic accepts a ceasefire in his fight with the KLA. International observers enter Kosovo.	**June**	Yugoslav and NATO generals sign agreement on withdrawal of Serb troops from Kosovo. Serb withdrawal begins. NATO air strikes halted. KFOR moves into Kosovo and UN takes over administration. Albanian refugees pour back.
October–December	USA fails to get a permanent settlement in Kosovo, and ceasefire collapses as KLA-Serb fighting increases.	**July**	Anti-government protests in Serbia. Rumours that Serbia plans to take over Montenegro.

GLOSSARY

Albania Balkan country inhabited largely by Albanians who have been in the region for over 2,000 years.

autonomy independence.

Balkans mountainous region to the east of the Adriatic Sea. It is home to many different ethnic groups.

colonization the process by which the Serb government encouraged Serb settlers to move to Kosovo to alter the ethnic balance there.

Democratic League of Kosovo (DLK) Led by Ibrahim Rugova, the DLK seeks greater independence for Kosovo by democratic means.

ethnic balance ratio of peoples of different ethnic origins. The balance in Kosovo is about 10 Albanians to each Serb.

ethnic cleansing process by which the Serbs tried to alter the ethnic balance in a region by getting rid of non-Serbs. It involved destruction of homes, forced emigration and, on occasion, mass murder.

European Union (EU) organization of Western European states founded in 1957 (as the European Economic Community) to promote peace, co-operation and prosperity.

guerrillas irregular soldiers who fight by ambush and hit-and-run raid rather than pitched battle.

KFOR NATO's peacekeeping force which entered Kosovo in June 1999.

Kosovo Liberation Army (KLA) extremist group dedicated to creating an independent Kosovo (or one united with other Albanian states) by driving the Serbs from Kosovo by force.

NATO North Atlantic Treaty Organization, a military organization set up by several Western nations in 1949 to defend themselves against Communism.

Orthodox Church the eastern branch of the Christian Church, originally based on Constantinople. It has branches in Russia, Greece, Serbia, Albania, etc.

Ottoman Empire huge Muslim empire established by the Ottoman Turks in the later Middle Ages. At its height it included the Balkans, North Africa and most of the Middle East. It was broken up after the First World War.

paramilitaries semi-official soldiers operating outside the army's command.

republic a state without a monarchy.

Serbia the Balkan state of the Serbs, an ethnic group descended from the ancient Slav peoples.

United Nations (UN) international organization set up in 1945 to preserve world peace, increase prosperity and safeguard human rights. Its most powerful committee is the Security Council.

US State Department section of US government that handles foreign affairs.

West shorthand term for the democratic nations of North America and Western Europe.

Yugoslavia multi-ethnic Balkan country set up in 1918. Most of its member states broke away during fighting in the early 1990s, leaving only Serbia (including Kosovo) and Montenegro.

INDEX

SOURCES

Websites

Information and many of the quotations in this book were taken from :

the DLK's Kosova Information Centre :
http://www.kosova.com

Kosova Crisis Centre (pro-Albanian):
http://www.alb-net.com

Albanian Information Service:
http://www.dardania.com

KLA:
http:/www.fas.org/irp/world/para/kla.htm
http:/www.kosovapress.com

Federal Government of Yugoslavia (FRY):
http:/www.gov.yu

Information on Serbia:
http:/www.serbia-info.com

NATO:
http://www.nato.int/kosovo

US information:
http://www.usia.gov/kosovo

UN High Commissioner on Refugees:
http://www.unhcr.ch/welcome.htm

Books
Amnesty International, *Yugoslavia: Ethnic Albanians: Trial by Truncheon*, London, 1994
P. Cohen, *Serbia's Secret War*, College Station, Texas, 1996
M. Glenny, *The Fall of Yugoslavia*, Penguin, 1993
B. Jelavich, *History of the Balkans*, 2 volumes, CUP, 1983
Noel Malcolm, *Bosnia A Short History*, Macmillan, London, 1996
Noel Malcolm, *Kosovo A Short History*, Macmillan, London, 1998
H. Poulton, *The Balkans*, London, 1993
L. Silber and A. Little, *The Death of Yugoslavia*, Penguin/BBC, 1996